Five Senses
Phonics

BOOK
2

Hunter Calder

A
FIVE SENSES
PUBLICATION

Five Senses Education Pty Ltd
2/195 Prospect Highway
Seven Hills NSW 2147 Australia
Phone   02 838 9265
Email   sevenhills@fivesenseseducation.com.au
Web   www.fivesenseseducation.com.au

Calder, Hunter
Five Senses Phonics Book 2
 978-1-76032-423-0

Contents

About the Author

Multiple award-winning author Hunter Calder has extensive experience as a reading teacher, consultant, teacher trainer and lecturer, both in Australia and overseas. He obtained a Master of Arts from the University of Sydney and a Master of Education from the University of New South Wales. His many publications include the acclaimed *Reading Freedom 2000* series and the *Excel Basic English* books. He also contributed to the *Literacy Planet* online program.

The *Five Senses Phonics* series of early literacy skills is his most recent series of phonics books and is the outcome of collaboration with the experienced people at Five Senses Education.

Introduction

Welcome to *Five Senses Phonics*, a carefully structured series of activity books for pre-readers and beginning readers at the important stage of their literacy acquisition. The Five Senses activity books are intended for use in a preschool setting, in the beginning school years, and for older students who are having difficulty learning to read.

Book 2 continues the development of the essential precondition of reading — phonemic awareness. Phonemic awareness refers to a student's ability to hear and work with sounds in spoken words. Students with good phonemic awareness skills know that words contain sequences of individual sounds. They know, for instance, the sounds 'b' - 'a' - 't' blend together to form the word 'bat'. Contemporary research tells us that students with good phonemic awareness skills go on to become competent readers. On the other hand, preschool age children and students in the early years at school who do not understand the relationship between spoken and written words are likely to develop literacy problems. Students who experience difficulty learning the skills of phonemic awareness may need the services of a specialised teacher trained in the development of auditory perception techniques.

The exercises are structured to allow the student to progressively attain competence in the skills of phonemic awareness. After completing Book 2, students are able to apply these skills to discriminate individual sounds in words. Students then progress onto Book 3 to acquire the basic phonics skills that develop good readers.

Student progress should regularly be monitored and evaluated after completing each level, using the Achievement Tests section which is specifically designed for teachers to assess effectiveness and so students can see the positive results of their learning experiences.

Instructions for Book 2

Pages 1–5 **Vowel and consonant sounds** — teach these sounds carefully until students reproduce them automatically.

Page 6 **Phonics Basic sight vocabulary** — these lists contain the basic sight words students need to work successfully with Phonics First. Teach the words list by list until they are mastered. Teach or revise the words as they are presented at the bottom of each page.

Pages 7–14 **Initial consonant sounds** — students say the words for the pictures and circle 'yes' if they begin with the same sound and 'no' if they don't.

Pages 15–22 **Terminal consonant sounds** — students say the words for the pictures and circle 'yes' if they end with the same sound and 'no' if they don't.

Pages 23–30 **Vowel discrimination** — students say the words for the pictures and circle the pictures containing the same vowel sound.

Pages 31–38 **Initial consonant sounds** — students say the words for the pictures and write the beginning sound they hear in the space provided.

Pages 39–46 **Terminal consonant sounds** — students say the words for the pictures and write the ending sound they hear in the space provided. Explain that even though a word like 'cave' ends with the letter 'e', the last sound they hear is 'v', so for 'cave' the letter to be circled is 'v'.

Pages 47–54 **Vowel discrimination** — students are to say the words for two pictures and circle 'yes' if they contain the same vowel sound and 'no' if they don't.

Pages 55–62 **Medial vowels** — students say the word for the picture and then write the vowel sound they hear in the space provided.

Pages 63–70 **Vowel-consonant blends** — students say the word for the picture and write the last two or three sounds they hear in the spaces provided.

Pages 71–79 **Alphabet knowledge** — students say the names for the letters. Ask them to say the names for both the upper case and lower case letter.

Pages 80–92 **Achievement tests** — students complete the tests to demonstrate mastery.

Sound Charts

Single Letter-Sound Correspondences: Vowels

Say the sounds for these letters.

a as in

e as in

i as in

o as in

U as in

Sound Charts

Single Letter-Sound Correspondences: Consonants

Say the sounds for these letters.

b   as   in

c   as   in

d   as   in

f   as   in

g   as   in

2

Sound charts

Say the sounds for these letters.

h   as   in

j   as   in

k   as   in

l   as   in

m   as   in

Sound charts

Say the sounds for these letters.

n   as   in

p   as   in

r   as   in

s   as   in

t   as   in

Sound charts

Say the sounds for these letters.

V   as   in

W   as   in

X   as   in

y   as   in

Z   as   in

5

Basic sight vocabulary

Learn these lists of sight words

a	in	and	saw	into	this
am	is	are	she	play	what
as	it	for	the	said	when
by	Mr	her	too	then	will
he	no	him	was	they	with
if	of	Mrs	why		
	on	not	yes		
		out	you		

Unit 1:1

Do the words **begin** with the same sound?
Circle 'yes' or 'no'.

    yes   no

    yes   no

    yes   no

    yes   no

    yes   no

a   am   as   (7)

Do the words **begin** with the same sound?
Circle 'yes' or 'no'.

8   a   am   as

Do the words **begin** with the same sound?
Circle 'yes' or 'no'.

    yes   no

    yes   no

    yes   no

    yes   no

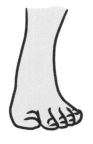    yes   no

a   am   as   9

Do the words **begin** with the same sound?
Circle 'yes' or 'no'.

    yes   no

    yes   no

    yes   no

    yes   no

    yes   no

Do the words **begin** with the same sound?
Circle 'yes' or 'no'.

  yes   no

  yes   no

  yes   no

  yes   no

  yes   no

a   am   as   (11)

Do the words **begin** with the same sound?
Circle 'yes' or 'no'.

  yes no

  yes no

  yes no

  yes no

  yes no

a   am   as

Do the words **begin** with the same sound?
Circle 'yes' or 'no'.

  yes no

  yes no

  yes no

  yes no

  yes no

a   am   as

Do the words **begin** with the same sound?
Circle 'yes' or 'no'.

    yes   no

    yes   no

    yes   no

    yes   no

    yes   no

(14)   a   am   as

Do the words **end** with the same sound?
Circle 'yes' or 'no'.

  yes no

  yes no

  yes no

  yes no

  yes no

by   he   if   in   15

Do the words **end** with the same sound?
Circle 'yes' or 'no'.

		yes	no
		yes	no
		yes	no
		yes	no
		yes	no

(16)   by   he   if   in

Do the words **end** with the same sound?
Circle 'yes' or 'no'.

  yes   no

  yes   no

  yes   no

  yes   no

  yes   no

by   he   if   in   (17)

Do the words **end** with the same sound?
Circle 'yes' or 'no'.

 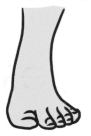   yes   no

    yes   no

    yes   no

    yes   no

    yes   no

(18)   by   he   if   in

Do the words **end** with the same sound?
Circle 'yes' or 'no'.

    yes   no

    yes   no

    yes   no

    yes   no

    yes   no

by   he   if   in   (19)

Do the words **end** with the same sound?
Circle 'yes' or 'no'.

  yes no

 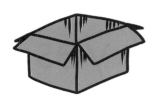 yes no

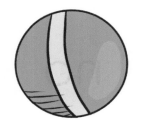  yes no

  yes no

  yes no

by he if in

Do the words **end** with the same sound?
Circle 'yes' or 'no'.

  yes no

  yes no

  yes no

  yes no

 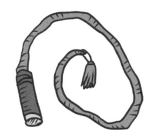 yes no

by   he   if   in   21

Do the words **end** with the same sound?
Circle 'yes' or 'no'.

  yes   no

  yes   no

  yes   no

  yes   no

  yes   no

(22)   by   he   if   in

Circle the two pictures with the same **vowel** sound.

by   he   if   in   23

Unit 3:2

Circle the two pictures with the same **vowel** sound.

is   it   Mr   no

Unit 3:3

Circle the two pictures with the same **vowel** sound.

is　　　　it　　　　Mr　　　　no　　　(25)

Circle the two pictures with the same **vowel** sound.

(26)   is   it   Mr   no

Unit 3:5

Circle the two pictures with the same **vowel** sound.

is   it   Mr   no   27

Unit 3:6

Circle the two pictures with the same **vowel** sound.

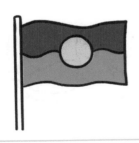  

(28)   is   it   Mr   no

Circle the two pictures with the same **vowel** sound.

is   it   Mr   no   29

Circle the two pictures with the same **vowel** sound.

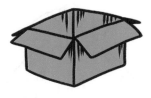

(30)   is   it   Mr   no

Write the **beginning** sound.

 __at

 __ap

 __og

 __an

 __at

 __ug

 __ug

 __ick

 __un

 __ips

of   on   and   are   (31)

Write the **beginning** sound.

 __et

 __ig

 __un

 __od

 __an

 __ap

 __ell

 __et

 __ip

 __uck

of   on   and   are

Write the **beginning** sound.

 __ug

 __lass

 __ill

 __ist

 __ing

 __an

 __ut

 __ilk

 __ock

 __un

of   on   and   are   (33)

Write the **beginning** sound.

 __at

 __oll

 __ate

 __ox

 __ell

 __and

 __eg

 __ing

 __en

 __oon

(34)   of   on   and   are

Write the **beginning** sound.

 __ask

 __led

 __ig

 __ruck

 __lag

 __oat

 __esk

 __lap

 __and

 __elt

of   on   and   are   35

Write the **beginning** sound.

 __est

 __ix

 __ress

 __ock

 __ank

 __eb

 __in

 __est

 __rog

 __op

of   on   and   are

Write the **beginning** sound.

 __amp

 __ite

 __atch

 __ool

 __ing

 __en

 __wim

 __lock

 __lock

 __rum

of   on   and   are   37

Write the **beginning** sound.

 __ish

 __ook

 __un

 __ate

 __ow

 __eaf

 __ine

 __top

 __ice

 __ave

of   on   and   are

Write the **ending** sound.

 clu__    nes__

 ca__e    sle__

 si__    cli__

 for__    bu__

 ba__ __    broo__

for   her   him   Mrs   39

Write the **ending** sound.

 pe__    bow__

 stam__    swi__

 sock__    sta__

 shar__    fro__

 kni__e    bir__

for   her   him   Mrs

Write the **ending** sound.

 cu__

 ca__

 bu__

 wa__e

 ba__

 fo__

 cra__

 be__

 pi__

 lea__

for　　　her　　　him　　　Mrs　　　41

Write the **ending** sound.

 ro__

 tu__

 ha__

 fi__e

 roo__

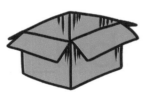 bo__

 do__

 tan__

 dru__

 snai__

for   her   him   Mrs

Write the **ending** sound.

 hoo__    han__

 ju__    je__

 dre__ __    hai__

 sto__    ru__

 ar__    be__ __

for   her   him   Mrs   43

Write the **ending** sound.

 lam__

 clow__

 bea__

 we__ __

 coo__

 le__

 hear__

 a__e

 cu__

 an__

(44)   for   her   him   Mrs

Write the **ending** sound.

 boo__

 tu__

 tai__

 sle__

 we__

 ba__

 gra__e

 crow__

 cro____

 ea__

for   her   him   Mrs   (45)

Write the **ending** sound.

 su__  hor__e

 fou__  shi __

 brea__  bow__

 mil__  fla__

 boo__  fo__

(46)   for   her   him   Mrs

Do the words have the same **vowel** sound?
Circle 'yes' or 'no'.

  yes   no

  yes   no

  yes   no

  yes   no

  yes   no

not   out   saw   she   47

Do the words have the same **vowel** sound?
Circle 'yes' or 'no'.

  yes no

  yes no

  yes no

 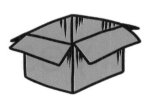 yes no

  yes no

(48) not   out   saw   she

Do the words have the same **vowel** sound?
Circle 'yes' or 'no'.

  yes no

  yes no

  yes no

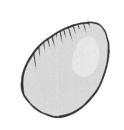  yes no

  yes no

not   out   saw   she   49

Do the words have the same **vowel** sound?
Circle 'yes' or 'no'.

  yes   no

  yes   no

  yes   no

  yes   no

  yes   no

(50)   not   out   saw   she

Do the words have the same **vowel** sound?
Circle 'yes' or 'no'.

 　　yes　　no

 　　yes　　no

 　　yes　　no

 　　yes　　no

 　　yes　　no

not　　　out　　　saw　　　she　　(51)

Do the words have the same **vowel** sound?
Circle 'yes' or 'no'.

    yes   no

    yes   no

 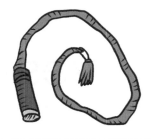   yes   no

    yes   no

    yes   no

not   out   saw   she

Do the words have the same **vowel** sound?
Circle 'yes' or 'no'.

    yes   no

    yes   no

    yes   no

    yes   no

    yes   no

not   out   saw   she   53

Do the words have the same **vowel** sound?
Circle 'yes' or 'no'.

    yes   no

    yes   no

    yes   no

    yes   no

    yes   no

not   out   saw   she

Write the **vowel** sound.

 b__x

 f__n

 p__n

 l__g

 h__t

 t__b

 b__d

 d__ll

 m__g

 b__t

the   too   was   why   55

Write the **vowel** sound.

 t_p

 f__x

 c__p

 k__ck

 cr__ss

 n__t

 p__g

 c__t

 w_b

 t_g

the   too   was   why

Write the **vowel** sound.

 r__d

 h__n

 d__ck

 c__p

 s__x

 s__ck

 v__n

 s__n

 b__ll

 w__g

the　　　too　　　was　　　why　　(57)

Write the **vowel** sound.

 h_ll

 b__g

 j_t

 d__g

 f__n

 l__ps

 l__ck

 r__n

 t_b

 w__ll

the   too   was   why

Write the **vowel** sound.

 c__p

 b__g

 t__sk

 l__mp

 m__lk

 b__lt

 v__st

 h__p

 bl__ck

 f__st

the   too   was   why   59

Write the **vowel** sound.

 n__st

 cl__b

 h__nd

 sw__m

 cl__ck

 fl__g

 st__mp

 t__nt

 cl__p

 fr__g

the   too   was   why

Write the **vowel** sound.

 dr__ss    r__ng

 st__mp    dr__m

 p__t    cr__b

 tr__nk    st__p

 sk__p    sl__d

the   too   was   why   61

Write the **vowel** sound.

 m__tch  f__sh

 sh__ll  r__ck

 th__ngs  cl__p

 tr__ck  d__sk

 k__ng  br__sh

the   too   was   why

Write the **last** sounds.

 c_ _ _

 d_ _ _ _

 p_ _ _ _

 s_ _ _

 s_ _ _

 t_ _ _

 b_ _ _ _

 j_ _ _

 p_ _ _

 b_ _ _

yes   you   into   play   63

Write the last sounds.

 n__ __

 w__ __

 z__ __

 l__ __

 d__ __

 f__ __

 b__ __

 c__ __

 t__ __

 r__ __

yes   you   into   play

Write the last sounds.

 f_ _ _

 cl_ _

 g_ _ _

 h_ _ _

 c_ _ _

 v_ _ _

 b_ _ _

 s_ _ _ _

 p_ _ _

 t_ _ _

yes   you   into   play   65

Write the last sounds.

 h_ _ _ _

 w_ _

 l_ _ _

 f_ _

 r_ _

 h_ _

 t_ _

 d _ _ _

 p_ _

 m_ _

yes   you   into   play

Write the first **two** sounds.

 __ __t

 __ __b

 __ __x

 __ __g

 __ __p

 __ __n

 __ __n

 __ __g

 __ __ck

 __ __s

said   then   they   this   67

Write the first **two** sounds.

 _ _ _n

 _ _ _ll

 _ _ _n

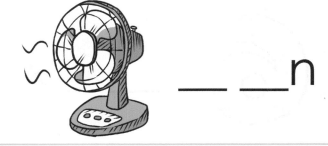 _ _ _n

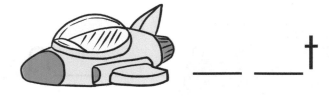 _ _ _t

 _ _ _b

 _ _ _ck

 _ _ _p

 _ _ _t

 _ _ _d

68   said   then   they   this

Write the first **two** sounds.

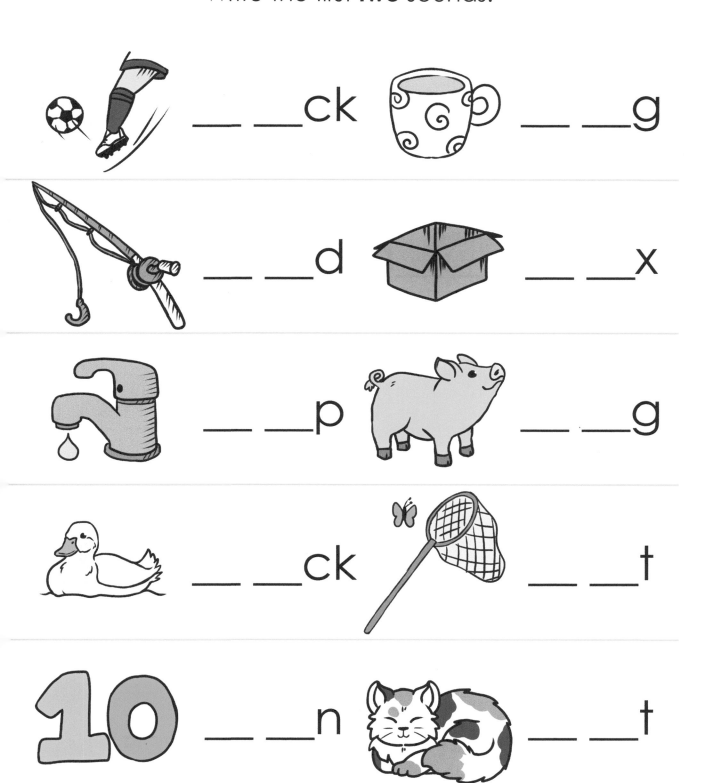

_ _ _ck   _ _ _g

_ _ _d   _ _ _x

_ _ _p   _ _ _g

_ _ _ck   _ _ _t

_ _ _n   _ _ _t

said   then   they   this   69

Unit 9:4

Write the first **two** sounds.

 _ _ _p

 _ _ _ll

 _ _ _n

 _ _ _ck

 _ _ _x

 _ _ _g

 _ _ _n

 _ _ _ll

 _ _ _ps

 _ _ _n

said   then   they   this

Say the names for the letters.

A a   B b   C c   D d   E e

F f   G g   H h   I i   J j

K k   L l   M m   N n   O o

P p   Q q   R r   S s   T t

U u   V v   W w   X x   Y y

Z z

what   when   will   with   71

Draw a line to match the **upper case** letter with the **lower case** letter.

O	q
P	t
S	v
X	y
U	o
Z	w
Q	x
T	p
Y	u
W	r
R	s
V	n
N	z

what   when   will   with

Draw a line to match the **upper case** letter with the **lower case** letter.

A	b
F	l
H	j
I	f
K	l
B	h
L	a
M	d
J	k
G	c
E	m
D	g
C	e

what   when   will   with

Draw a line to match match the **lower case** letter with the **upper case** letter.

b	N
c	L
h	S
g	O
k	Q
l	G
q	C
n	H
s	Y
x	B
w	X
o	W
y	K

what   when   will   with

Draw a line to match match the **lower case** letter with the **upper case** letter.

d	P
f	T
a	M
i	A
m	U
j	E
r	Z
p	F
u	D
t	I
z	R
v	J
e	V

what   when   will   with   (75)

Look at the **upper case** letter in the box.
Circle the same **lower case** letter.

X	a	b	c	x	e
B	d	c	e	z	b
E	e	y	d	x	a
F	w	f	l	e	x
D	f	d	z	y	c
I	i	g	v	w	f
K	u	t	k	i	h
L	v	l	u	h	g
N	s	t	j	i	n
R	n	k	l	q	r
O	r	j	o	s	k
T	m	l	p	t	o
U	u	n	o	m	p

76 what   when   will   with

Look at the **upper case** letter in the box.
Circle the same **lower case** letter.

W	l	w	y	b	z
A	x	z	w	y	a
C	v	c	a	u	z
G	u	v	g	d	a
J	c	t	s	f	j
H	h	s	e	t	b
P	q	e	r	p	h
M	g	d	b	r	m
S	s	j	o	p	g
Q	f	q	p	o	i
Z	n	l	z	i	m
V	k	m	v	h	n
Y	d	k	l	y	j

what   when   will   with   (77)

Look at the **lower case** letter in the box.
Circle the same **upper case** letter.

j	Y	B	A	J	W
a	C	A	Z	X	Y
q	X	C	Q	V	B
d	V	E	T	A	D
s	W	D	S	C	U
l	T	L	R	F	G
i	U	F	E	S	I
n	R	I	H	N	P
f	S	G	F	Q	H
t	T	Q	J	O	I
w	N	K	P	J	W
e	M	Z	E	L	N
z	K	L	Z	M	O

what   when   will   with

Look at the **lower case** letter in the box.
Circle the same **upper case** letter.

m	W	M	C	B	H
h	H	C	X	Z	B
b	D	A	B	Y	E
o	J	O	Z	E	U
v	D	I	F	V	A
c	E	T	Y	C	K
y	Y	G	X	L	S
k	H	K	M	R	W
p	N	Q	P	V	I
u	U	P	K	T	O
r	J	O	P	R	U
g	I	G	M	J	R
x	S	L	X	N	Q

what   when   will   with   (79)

Achievement tests

The Five Senses Phonics Achievement Tests complement each book in the Five Senses Phonics series. They are specifically designed to enable teachers to ensure that what has been taught remains current in the student's repertoire of skills. They can then identify areas that need reteaching or reinforcement.

The format of each Five Senses Phonics Achievement Test is identical to the equivalent book so students encounter activities with which they are familiar. Each test evaluates skills and sight words students have been taught. The careful design of the tests, ensures that the monitoring of progress is a positive and non-threatening exercise.

For ease of administration, the tests are photocopiable. The class record sheets and student record sheets allow the teacher to scan student performance on an individual or whole class basis. Taken as a group, the tests give a running record of each student's skill acquisition of the phonic hierarchy. Teachers who teach reading systematically and record student progress methodically will find the Five Senses Phonics First Achievement Tests an indispensable part of their teaching routine.

How to use these tests

The Five Senses Phonics Achievement Tests are intended to be an encouraging record of progress, not an intimidating assessment. The tests can be administered to individual students or the entire class. Allow approximately 30 minutes to complete each test.

Each group of tests contains one or two sight vocabulary tests. If administering the test to the class as a whole, have individual students read groups of sight words, then ask the class to read all sight words together. Keep watch for children who are having trouble, and test them later individually.

Maintain a positive attitude while administering the tests, and reward success with stickers, stamps and merit certificates. To attain mastery students should obtain at least 80 marks out of a possible 100. Any areas in the Test that indicate weakness should be retaught and then reinforced.

Test record sheet

Student .... Date...

Page	Test		
82	1	Initial consonants	/ 5
83	2	Terminal consonants	/ 5
84	3	Medial vowels	/ 5
85	4	Writing initial consonants	/10
86	5	Writing terminal consonants	/10
87	6	Discriminating vowel sounds	/ 5
88	7	Writing medial vowels	/10
89	8	Writing vowel-consonant blends	/10
90	9	Writing consonant-vowel blends	/10
91–92	10	Alphabet knowledge	/30

Total /100

Do the words **begin** with the same sound?
Circle **yes** or **no**.

    yes   no

    yes   no

    yes   no

    yes   no

    yes   no

Score   / 5

Test 2:2

Do the words **end** with the same sound?
Circle **yes** or **no**.

    yes   no

    yes   no

    yes   no

    yes   no

    yes   no

Score / 5

83

Test 2:3

Circle the two pictures with the same **vowel** sound.

84

Score / 5

Test 2:4

Write the **beginning** sound.

 __at

 __ug

 __at

 __ing

 __ock

 __est

 __ork

 __ruck

 __uck

 __ix

Score [/ 10]

85

Test 2:5

Write the **ending** sound.

 cu__

 dru__

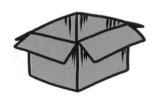 bo__

 bir__

 lea__

 hoo__

 tu__

 dre__ __

 ca__e

 we__ __

Score / 10

Test 2:6

Discriminating vowel sounds

Do the words have the same **vowel** sound?
Circle **yes** or **no**.

  yes   no

  yes   no

  yes   no

  yes   no

  yes   no

Score [/ 5]

87

Test 2:7

Write the **vowel** sound.

 l__g

 c__p

 cr__b

 r__ck

 s__n

 st__mp

 p__g

 bl__ck

 k__ng

 j__t

Score 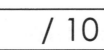 / 10

Test 2:8

Write the **last** sounds.

 b_ _ _

 p_ _ _

 l_ _ _ _

 l_ _ _

 r_ _ _

 f_ _ _

 b_ _ _

 n_ _ _

 f_ _ _

 f_ _ _

Score ⬚ / 10

89

Write the first **two** sounds

 _ _ _ p

 _ _ _ t

 _ _ n

 _ _ _ d

 _ _ _ g

 _ _ _ ck

 _ _ _ t

 _ _ g

 _ _ _ p

 _ _ _ n

Score / 10

Test 2:10

Look at the **upper case** letter in the box.
Circle the same **lower case** letter.

U	u	n	m	p	o
T	m	l	p	t	q
O	r	j	o	s	k
R	n	k	l	q	r
N	d	t	n	j	i
L	v	l	u	h	g
K	u	t	k	i	h
P	p	g	v	w	f
D	f	d	z	y	c
F	w	f	l	e	x
E	e	y	d	x	a
B	d	c	e	z	b
A	x	z	w	y	a
H	h	s	e	t	b
Y	d	k	l	y	j

Score [/ 15]

91

Look at the **lower case** letter in the box.
Circle the same **upper case** letter.

z	K	L	Z	M	O
e	M	Z	E	L	N
w	N	K	P	J	W
i	T	Q	J	O	I
f	S	G	F	Q	H
n	R	L	H	N	P
o	J	O	Z	E	U
l	T	L	R	F	G
s	W	D	S	C	U
d	V	E	T	A	D
q	X	C	Q	V	B
a	C	A	Z	X	Y
j	J	B	A	Y	W
e	E	T	Y	C	K
x	S	L	X	N	Q

Score / 15